I AM
BREAD
BROKEN

I AM BREAD BROKEN

A Spirituality
for the Catechist

HOWARD J. HUBBARD

A Crossroad Herder Book
The Crossroad Publishing Company
New York

I Am Bread Broken was first presented at the Eastern
Religious Education Conference in Washington, D.C.,
on February 24, 1995. The transcript of the
presentation has been edited for publication.

1996

The Crossroad Publishing Company
370 Lexington Avenue, New York, NY 10017

Printed in the United States of America

Library of Congress Catalog Card No.: 96-83572
ISBN 0-8245-1575-7

Contents

Foreword   7

5

Part Two

THE QUALITIES
OF THE CATECHIST

Foreword

I T IS with great apprehension and reservation that I speak to catechists about spirituality because really it is you the catechists in our parishes and schools who from your own lived experience know much more about the topic and are much more qualified to reflect upon it than I.

So let me begin by very simply, yet very sincerely expressing gratitude and appreciation to you catechists for the extraordinary and indispensable ministry of faith formation you exercise in the church.

Yours indeed is a challenging role, namely,

that of imparting religious values and of fostering an understanding of faith in our secularistic age, of preparing our young and adults for the sacraments of baptism, confirmation, Eucharist, reconciliation, and marriage and of passing on the precious heritage of our Catholic Christian tradition.

It is a role that is frequently misunderstood, occasionally maligned, and fraught with a plethora of logistic hassles presupposing knowledge and skills related to curriculum content, pedagogy, and administration, and requiring of you the wisdom of Solomon as you seek to address and resolve the ofttimes conflicting expectations of pastors, parents, teachers, and students alike.

Yet it is a mission and a ministry that is vitally essential to the church and one of enormous importance as you set the tone for how the Good News is proclaimed, reflected upon, discussed, and put into practice through prayer, worship, and service.

For very often it is you who have the most personal contact with the mainstream of the parish. And the vision you articulate to teachers, parents, and youth, the curriculum and textbooks you recommend for classroom use, the sacramental policies you help to shape, and the adult education you impart either to teachers or to parents in sacramental preparation programs have more influence on the religious development of people than anything else that occurs in the life of the church.

So I salute you who are the frontline evangelists in our church for your dedication and commitment, for your vision and sense of the church, for your patience in working with inadequate resources, at low wages, in a role that is largely unsung, and above all for the personal witness you offer to how the Christian life is lived in practice.

Yes, you are truly instruments of hope in an age of uncertainty and despair; you are heralds of that ageless wisdom of self-forgetfulness, of dying to self and living a life of love and service on behalf of others in our yuppie age of narcissism and individualism, and you are bearers of that two thousand-year-old tradition of our Catholic Christian heritage rooted firmly as it is in the Scriptures and in the church's liturgical and sacramental life in a world whose memory seems not to extend beyond yesterday's headlines.

Part One

THE CALL
OF THE CATECHIST

The Crisis of
Spirituality

I T IS INTERESTING TO NOTE that there is a
renewed quest for spirituality in our society. Just check out the barometers in the
cultural marketplace. Bookstores are lined
with spiritual missives, ranging from Pope
John Paul II's *Crossing the Threshold of
Hope*, to James Redfield's spiritual novel
The Celestine Prophecy, to Kathleen Nor-
ris's *Dakota, a Spiritual Biography*. Music
stores feature best-selling Gregorian chants
by the Benedictine monks of Santo Domingo

de Silos. Hollywood salts its scripts with divine reference and afterlife experiences. Celebrities as different as tennis star Andre Agassi and playwright David Mamet tell interviewers how they found God in their lives, while Newt Gingrich and others have pushed school prayer onto the national agenda and *Newsweek* magazine has run a cover story on the Search for the Sacred.

The reason for this renewed interest in things spiritual, I believe, is that the crisis of our age is a crisis of spirituality. We have lost a sense of the transcendent; we have lost the art of contemplation; we have failed in our efforts to integrate liturgy and work, prayer and service, faith and action. To be sure, we have moved away from that monastic approach to spirituality that dominated the life of the church for many centuries, but we are still in the midst of developing an authentic apostolic spirituality, one that enables us to harmonize our work and our prayer,

one that enables us to be doers who contem-
plate, one that enables us to reflect upon the
wonder of the Father's creation, the beauty
of the Redeemer's love, and the pulsating
presence of God's spirit within us, and then
to translate that reflection into words and
deeds that speak clearly and meaningfully to
contemporary realities.

God's Call in Your Life

THIS, MY FRIENDS, is precisely the type of spirituality you are called to cultivate as catechists: a spirituality that must be rooted in the call that you have received and in the word of God you are privileged to proclaim and interpret.

Regarding the concept of call, it is important to note that the Christian life is truly a life of call and response. First and foremost must come the call. And it is God and God alone who initiates this call. It is the Lord who plants the seed in our heart, it is the Lord who whispers the divine word into our ear, and it is the Lord God who breathes the lifegiving spirit into our being.

But this planting, whispering, and breathing can either fall upon closed minds, hardened hearts, and deaf ears or upon open minds, searching hearts, and receptive ears.

In the case of so many catechists it has been the latter. God's call in your life has not gone unheeded. Rather it touched you at baptism, it moved you and drew you to become actively involved in your faith community, and it has inspired you to accept the commission of your bishop and pastor to be a minister of the word to God's people in your diocese and parish. Remember, then, as the National Catechetical Directory makes abundantly clear, your ministry as a catechist is truly a call from the Lord. "You did not choose me, I chose you." These words of Jesus addressed in the first instance to the apostles at the Last Supper meal offer a profound message for catechists as well.

For God has indeed called and chosen you for the ministry you exercise. What dignity this gives to your catechetical activity, the dignity of knowing that as a catechist you are truly responding to a divine call. And what a consolation as well, especially when you are tempted to feel unworthy of the awesome responsibility that your catechetical ministry entails. It is then that you must remember that you indeed are called and chosen. Earthen vessels? No doubt. Weak instruments? Of course. Doubting Thomases or fretting Marthas sometimes? Yes. Fainthearted in adversity and failing in love like Peter? Inevitably. But with all of this you have been called and chosen and this makes all the difference in the world.

Word and Flesh

YOUR SPIRITUALITY as a catechist must be rooted in the word of God at whose service your ministry is placed. From the very beginning of the history of salvation it has been the word of God that has brought the community of the Lord's covenant into being and nourished its existence. The creation of Israel from a mere multitude to the people of God came about through the proclamation of God's word. Down through the centuries, that word — received and recorded by the patriarchs, prophets, and psalmists — molded, formed, and shaped the Israelites and sustained them throughout their turbulent history as a nomadic people, subject to the slings and arrows of their enemies. Finally after the Egyptian exile and wandering through the desert God's word led them to the promised land.

However, it was the word made flesh, Jesus Christ, who made known the fullness of God's revelation and established that new and eternal covenant that to this day enlightens us and guides our destiny as a chosen race, a royal priesthood, a people the Lord God has made his own.

And the mystery of the word of God is that it is a living word, which has special significance for you as catechists. For when you bring the lessons of our Christian faith rooted in God's word to your hearers, to your students, you do more than recall historical events of the past. Rather you bring the Scriptures alive to those gathered to receive it, a word that has the power to touch lives and to change hearts.

The aim of your proclamation of God's word, in other words, is not to force an ancient story on a modern community, a stale document taken from the sterile archives of history; it is rather to make the word of God actual and present to your hearers as a ferment within the community. For God's word is a living word that does what it says and that has the power to bring about what it proclaims.

So your spirituality as catechists must be rooted firmly in the call that you have received and in the word that you are challenged to unfold.

What You Have to Offer

=== ❦ ===

PLEASE KNOW that what you have to offer as catechists is precisely what our contemporary society so desperately needs. Polls show, for example, that while Americans, including our Catholic people, remain persons of faith, very often their beliefs do not significantly affect their major life decisions. Their relationship with God is often marginalized and isolated from their relationship with self and the world. Yet with all of this, there is a hunger on the part of this generation for an inner life; people are searching for security and certainty amid the complexities and frustrations of contemporary society. They want to know how to find God and to be assured that God loves them and will not abandon them in the midst of their life's struggles.

And this, I believe, is one of the essential and vital roles you have to play as catechists: to lead people into an ever more intimate contact with God. As catechists you are called to be teachers, speaking to people about the ultimate concern, which is God's passionate, unconditional, and excessive love. You must hold up to the people of God the images, stories, and symbols of salvation that lie at the heart of our Catholic Christian tradition and then make these speak to contemporary realities. In particular you must tell the story of Jesus and make the connection between his life and message and the struggles, sorrows, hopes, joys, and expectations of people today.

People Seek

=◊=

YES, what people need and want most today is a deeper understanding of Jesus,
the Christ. They want to know, feel, and experience Jesus and to see how the story of
Jesus intertwines with their own.

As Father Patrick Carroll suggests in an
excellent article in *Church* magazine, few
parishioners today evidence a passionate interest in biblical exegesis, but they do have a
deep longing for meaning in their lives. They
want to know that what life is about has to
do with saving and being saved, freeing and
being set free, loving and being loved, and

that all this counts for something. And the
story of Jesus — when it becomes our own
story — provides such meaning.

To most people it matters little that Jesus
walked on water some two thousand years
ago and that Peter walked with him. What
matters to them, however, is to know that
when they are sinking, this Jesus in whom
they put their faith and trust will lift them
up. What matters to them is whether they
can muster the courage to step out of the
boat and into the storm. What matters to
them is whether they can invite others to take
bold new steps into unfamiliar territory, with
confidence in this same Jesus.

Part Two

THE QUALITIES
OF THE CATECHIST

Entering
the Mystery
of Jesus

A S TEACHERS, then, you must enter the mystery of Jesus, seeing how his life, his words, his temptations, his choices, his facing death, and his overcoming death relate to the demands of the day, to the needs of God's people and to the fears of the nations.

If, however, you are to develop a spirituality that enables you to be heralds, bearers, and interpreters of God's word and especially the Jesus story, then, you must strive to integrate ten important qualities into your life and catechetical ministry.

1. A People of Vision

FIRST, AS CATECHISTS you must be people of vision, men and women who believe in the creative and renewing power of the Holy Spirit, who constantly challenges us to risk the unpredictable, to believe in the heretofore unseen and then have the courage to make such a reality. To be visionary leaders in today's church, in other words, means we must be liberated from calculated plans, systems, and patterns that promise us security and pat solutions to life's problems so that we can allow the Holy Spirit to move us where the Spirit wills, that Holy Spirit who ever moves us into the uncharted courses of our unpredictable God, who is predictable only in the call to lead us from where we may have comfortably settled.

This need for visionary leadership in today's church was brought home to me very powerfully by an essay I read in a book by Robert Greenleaf entitled *Servant Leadership*. In assessing the situation of the Catholic Church in the United States, Greenleaf stated:

> The Catholic Church in the United States is a minority religion, but I regard it as potentially the largest single force for good within our society. However, the Catholic Church fails to realize its potential for good in today's society, because, I believe, it is seen as predominantly a negative force. The issues on which the Church is in opposition, such as birth control, abortion, euthanasia, divorce and communism are specific

and precisely defined and the actions of the Church here are vigorous and sustained. The issues, however, on which the church is affirmative such as peace, justice and charity, are broad, idealistic generalities and the Church's actions in this regard are sporadic and imprecise.

Greenleaf continues:

I respect the Church for opposing those social practices which it believes to be wrong even though I don't always agree with its judgment. But unfortunately all one can do with opposition is to stop or prevent something. Yes, one must oppose those things that one believes wrong, but one cannot lead from a predominantly negative posture. One can lead an institution or a total society only by strong, sharply aimed affirmative action. As a non-Catholic, I was lifted up by Pope John XXIII's regime, because an affirmative building leadership seemed to be emerging and this gave new hope for the world.

Greenleaf's observations, I think, underscore the need for visionary leadership within the church. Far too often, we as a Christian community present to a world starved for hope, not so much, as St. Paul proclaims, "the image of a people sure of who we are and what we stand for," but rather the image of people more cowed by fear than sustained by hope.

As catechists, therefore, you must strive to be people of vision, people who are willing to take risks and explore new frontiers. Otherwise you will leave the leadership role in our church and society to others or, as is more likely to be the case, our church and society will become leaderless.

2. Deep and Abiding Trust

=== 🔥 ===

SECOND, AS CATECHISTS you must manifest a deep and abiding trust in the Lord and in God's providence, in a God who never promised us instant success and who frequently writes our history with crooked lines.

Since Vatican Council II the church has been experiencing a period of transition. It has been a time for building and rebuilding, a time characterized by much confusion and turmoil. At times, in the midst of such changes there can emerge the temptation to become impatient, to lose sight of the fact that the renewal of the church or the renewal of catechetics is not a romp for a few years of intensive work, but a long, hard, arduous process that will undoubtedly stretch beyond our lifetime. That is why we need patient endurance to carry us through the many winters that it takes to renew attitudes and structures. That is why we must strive to avoid the pitfall of "instant antiquity," the pitfall of thinking that the problems, the crises and challenges we are currently experiencing are the most serious crises and problems ever encountered. This attitude arises because we have simply not experienced the pain of other challenges, of other crises or other periods of history.

If, therefore, you are to avoid discouragement and disillusionment in your ministry, then you must have a vision of life that is rooted in trust in God's providence and in the cleansing discipline of historical perspective, a vision of life that recognizes that we live in a church and society where there are few areas that are all black and white, but where various shades of gray predominate.

If you are committed to ministering in such a church and society, then you must be willing to accept the confusion, uncertainty, and turmoil that abound therein and be willing to tolerate imperfection while seeking to change it. This is not to lose your ideals nor to compromise your values but to live like human beings in a world where the full force of Christ's resurrection and the work of the Holy Spirit as yet have not been felt. Yes, we constantly live in the balance between the cross and the resurrection, on the one hand weeping over the plight of Jerusalem and on the other hand joyful because of an Easter victory that assures us of the possibilities of tomorrow and challenges us to celebrate a future that shapes our present moment in history.

3. Ecclesial Perspective

THIRD, AS CATECHISTS you must have a strong sense of ecclesial perspective. By that I mean you must have a sound historical, philosophical, and theological understanding of where the church as a community has been, is presently, and will be in the future. This sense of ecclesial perspective is important for two reasons. First, it will help you better understand those who come from a model or perspective of the church different from the one you have, so that you can accept these persons where they are, just as Jesus accepted people where they were, and then as he did strive to lead them gently and sensitively to a renewed understanding of what it means to be God's people.

I mention this because, at times, I have observed catechists who have become so caught up with the newest theological and scriptural insights or with the latest liturgical innovations, that they trample upon or become hypercritical of people who are as yet unaware of or not ready for such advances. Or they become intolerant of a diversity of ecclesiologies, spiritualities, and ministerial viewpoints within the church. Therefore, you must develop a sense of ecclesial perspective that enables you to be patient with people and institutions that seem to change only slowly.

A second important reason for an ecclesial perspective is that you be aware of the corporate character of the church and the collective mission you have as ministers in the church. I point this out because as a bishop I have observed firsthand what Father Phillip Murnion, the priest-sociologist from the archdiocese of New York, has documented by his research, namely, a tendency on the part of some to look upon the ministry they exercise as a license for private practice, a license to do one's own thing, to carve out a particular work or apostolate that is personally satisfying and to resist or neglect aspects of ministry that do not fit within their personal framework.

You catechists must recognize that you are part of the universal church, of a diocesan community and of a parish family, and you must be responsive to the needs, priorities, and policies of that wider church beyond your own personal vision.

You, in other words, must see your particular ministry as part of the overall ministry of the universal and diocesan church, not as a separate isolated entity.

As a corollary to having a strong sense

3. Ecclesial Perspective

of ecclesial perspective, I would suggest that as catechists you must be persons who are supportive of the policies of the church, community, or institution that you serve and cooperative with others who hold positions of leadership and responsibility. I mention this because I am convinced that backbiting, foot-dragging, and the overt or covert undermining of authority have been among the greatest problems that have confronted us in our post-conciliar church.

Please do not misinterpret what I say. By loyalty I don't mean blind obedience, unthinking docility, or sycophant-like submission. We've had far too much of that in the past with rather disastrous consequences. Neither by loyalty would I in any way want to stifle the prophetic voice within the life of the church, because such is always needed for ongoing growth and renewal. However, within this context, there is still need for loyalty. For while as catechists you must share your opinions, champion your causes, and make known your dissent, all of this must be submitted to the discernment process within the total community and to the decision-making structures present therein. And once decisions have been made and policies formulated, then these need to be implemented and supported with a degree of enthusiasm, decisiveness, and conviction. Otherwise it is undermining to the overall life and mission of the church. A spirit of loyalty, harmony, and mutual support then is essential for catechists and the natural fruit of a true ecclesial perspective.

4. The Gift of Your Real Self

FOURTH, AS CATECHISTS you must be comfortable with your humanity. Catechists are commissioned as teachers in the church and have the responsibility to teach what the church teaches. As I have just suggested, you work within the context of a universal church, a diocese, a parish, and structure within that parish. To do so at times this will mean sacrificing some of your own ideas, thoughts, insights, and approaches for the good of the whole. But this does not presuppose the destruction of your identity or personality. Rather as catechists you must allow your own identity, your own personality, your own humanity to emerge in your ministry. The personal touch is far more important than any robotic performance you may give.

Survey after survey reveals that people want catechists to be warm, sensitive, understanding human beings. The qualities I hear people talk most enthusiastically about in describing those catechists who have greatly influenced their lives are the following: they are friendly; they are kind; they really care; they seem to understand; they truly believe what they teach; they acknowledge their own difficulties and struggles.

That is why as catechists it is so important that you be in touch with your own humanity, that you simply be yourself. For discovering and believing in one's self is a major human task in a world disorientated by sin. Remember, your ministry as a catechist arises from the need of the community, and what the community most needs today in those who minister is not a walking theology manual but sensitive and caring human beings who are willing to share their humanity with others by being there in the thick of things, in the midst of their life's struggles, and by paying loving attention to them.

Recently, at our retreat for catechists, one catechist said, "My ministry is the ministry of interruptions." How true! If, therefore, you are not willing to share the gift of your real self with others, or if you hide behind your role or your professional skills, then you will never be truly successful as a catechist and you will never know the real joy and the intense pain of being a genuine herald of the Good News.

I know personally how difficult it can be to truly let your humanity come shining through your ministry. For example, before becoming bishop in the diocese of Albany, I worked in the inner city. During that period I had no problem at all in responding to people's physical or social needs, in talking to all kinds of groups about the theological imperative of social ministry, or in delivering homilies about God, prayer, the Eucharist, and the sacraments. When, however, it came time to speak with another person on a one-to-one basis about the Christian life, especially if that person did not initiate the conversation, I literally froze, feeling that this would be unprofessional and coercive, or feeling just plain awkward and uncomfortable in the situation.

On the one hand, I rationalized that I was trying to avoid the trap of "rice Christianity," namely, offering people assistance on the condition that they accept our faith, but in my heart of hearts I realized that I was allowing my own self-image and my own fear of human respect to get in the way of my baptismal commitment and ordination responsibility to preach the Good News of Jesus Christ both in season and out of season.

To offer another example, a few years ago I attended a workshop on evangelization. One of the exercises was to select someone else in the room, preferably someone you did not know well, and share with that person who Jesus is for you. While everyone in the room was a committed Catholic Christian, mostly priests, and while the sharing took place on a one-to-one basis, not in front of the entire group, I found it very awkward and difficult to share in this fashion.

This awkwardness in sharing very personal faith or prayer experiences with others, apart from our formal presentations, I believe, creates for us in the Catholic community a great difficulty in coping with the growing trend toward fundamentalism within our society. It may also be the answer as to why our efforts at evangelization at times have been so impoverished. Therefore, it is important that as catechists you develop a greater facility and comfortableness in sharing your faith and prayer experiences with others.

5. *A People of Joy*

F IFTH, AS CATECHISTS you must be people of joy. If there is one thing that has been notably absent in our post-conciliar church, it is a positive, upbeat, and optimistic spirit. For example, in the process of implementing the norms and reforms of the Second Vatican Council, of combating the growing secularization that engulfs us, and of coping with the diverse issues that have been so much a part of contemporary Catholicism — issues like birth control, married clergy, and women priests, the exercise of authority in the church, as well as of addressing the problems created by clergy sexual misconduct, declining vocations to the priesthood and religious life, and the closing or consolidation of parishes and schools — we have lost or at least have tended to downplay that sense of joy that is the hallmark of the Christian life.

It is imperative, therefore, that as catechists you be joyful ministers of the Good News. Gloomy Guses or Sourpuss Sals have no place in contemporary catechetical ministry. Your presence, your gestures, your words must radiate the message: "I'm delighted to be here; I'm delighted to be with you; I'm delighted to be a herald of the Good News." And it is indeed good news that you are called and sent to proclaim. Therefore, smile; be happy; show that there is joy in what you are doing, for the effectiveness of your catechetical ministry depends upon it.

As catechists you must also have a sense of humor. Very often we who minister in the church can look upon humor as frivolous, undignified, or unbecoming the grand scheme of the divine that we are privileged to represent. Or because we are often dealing with serious issues or with people having serious problems, we can tend to become overly dour.

That is why it is important that we be able to step back to gain the balance, the proportion, and the sense of perspective to cope with the incongruities of life and to realize that these incongruities need not defeat us. Rather, as the resurrection of Jesus so well proclaims, ultimate victory over forces that seem insurmountable is truly possible.

And a sense of humor enables us to gain this perspective. Note well that the humor of which I speak has nothing to do with laughing and telling jokes; for the world is full of people who laugh and tell jokes but who have no sense of humor. Rather, genuine humor, like a true sense of humility, involves a ruthless honesty about oneself without any pretense or show. It deals with those surprises that upset the way we think things ought to be, and it lightens the heaviness associated with hurt. Humor doesn't deny hurt, but it becomes the vehicle through which anger, defiance, and pain can be handled constructively.

I hope, then, that you catechists will develop a sense of humor that enables you to laugh at yourself, so that you can avoid that anxiety or uptightness that can impede your ministerial effectiveness and that can make it much more difficult for others to recognize God's presence in your life and your ministry.

6. The Spirit of Wonder and Awe

SIX, AS CATECHISTS you must be flexible and open to change. Ministry in the church today is pretty much the same as it was in apostolic times: to teach the word, to build up Christian community, and to serve humankind. But how this is done, where the stress falls, where the emphasis is placed changes. It can never remain the same; it can never become frozen. Ministry in the church is the function of the church's mission. And the mission of the church is not to some abstract humanity but to the concrete world, to these pulsing people with changing needs and changing life situations, with different colors and smells, with different problems and pressures, with different hopes, expectations, and frustrations than those experienced by previous generations.

Given this reality, then, one of the most important qualities that you as catechists must have is to develop the ability to learn, to grow, to adapt, the capacity to turn a corner, to change an attitude, to move on. In celebrating the sacrament of confirmation I am frequently struck by the words of the prayer recited over the candidates: "Give them the spirit of wisdom and understanding; the spirit of right judgment and courage; the spirit of knowledge and reverence; and fill them with the spirit of wonder and awe in your presence." What we need in today's church is more people who have this sense of wonder and awe, because people who are filled with the sense of wonder and awe can never limit themselves to maintenance or to the status quo. Instead they are constantly celebrating, rejoicing, and moving on because the mysteries they touch are so vast and so beautiful. There is always the possibility for new insights and fresh perspectives. There are always new colors and shades to be added to the landscape. It is important then that as catechists you be filled with the sense of wonder and awe, ever open to new challenges, to new vistas and horizons.

As a corollary to being flexible and open to change you must also be committed to ongoing education and formation. You must make time for reading, listening to tapes, and attending retreats, workshops, lectures, and courses that will keep you abreast of what is happening in Scripture, liturgy, moral and dogmatic theology, and contemporary pastoral practice. And in keeping abreast you must seek to gain a balanced understanding of contemporary pastoral and theological issues, one that is fully in accord with the mind and heart of the church, and not just to follow the pet theories of your favorite guru or latch on to the latest fad.

Indeed, as Cardinal Godfried Danneels of Belgium has pointed out, the intellectual dimension of your ministry as catechists is more relevant and more important today than ever before. For the cardinal suggests that the challenge of our age is to create a dialogue between religion and science, faith and culture. But if this is to happen, then our efforts at evangelization must have a strong intellectual and philosophical basis; our catechesis must have a sound cognitive content, and apologetics must again become part and parcel of the life of the church. We must, in other words, develop new theological language that speaks to modern men and women and that ensures a fresh airing for the Christian revelation. And this is your role and responsibility as catechists. If you fail to do this, then you will stunt your own personal and professional growth; you will become prime candidates for drop-out or burnout, and worst of all you will shortchange the people you have been sent to serve.

7. Theology of the Cross

SEVENTH, AS CATECHISTS you must adopt a theology of the cross. This is particularly important in this age of instant gratification in which we find ourselves. We in the United States, in this latter half of the twentieth century, have been sold and, to a large extent, have bought a bill of goods. This bill of goods tells us that pain and suffering, that tension and anxiety, that discomfort of any sort need not exist and that life at all times and under every circumstance is meant to be pleasurable and comfortable. In other words, we have been convinced that for every pain there is an antidote, for every depression there is a mood reverser, for every bit of discomfort there is some new magic formula that is going to alter our life's situation.

However, as we all know from experience, life just isn't like that. There is always need for discipline and sacrifice in our lives. This is one of the great mysteries of our faith, the mystery of the cross.

Thus, as catechists, you must recognize and appreciate that the cross must be an integral and essential of the Christian life — of your life: the cross of heralding a message that is countercultural and that, consequently, will be frequently ridiculed, scorned, and rejected; the cross of serving in a church that is still in the throes of transition, where age-old moorings have been cut, and where we are experiencing the tension and stress of birthing new ministerial models and approaches; the cross of giving up some ideas that once seemed unchangeable or shedding attitudes that used to provide security; the cross of being misunderstood and misjudged, but also the cross of not seeing clearly and thus of misunderstanding and misjudging others; the cross of being patient and kind, even when humanly speaking there seems to be every reason to fight back; the cross of showing compassion to others when precious little compassion is shown in return.

Yes, accepting these and other crosses too numerous, too unpredictable, and too personal to mention, like a job loss, the death of a loved one, a child gone wrong, an alcoholic family member, a serious illness, must be an inevitable part of your spirituality as a catechist.

8. Instruments of Tenderness and Mercy

EIGHTH, AS CATECHISTS you must be instruments of tenderness and mercy. Recently, both Father John Catoir of the Christopher Movement and Bishop John McCarthy of Austin, Texas, have pointed out that there seems to be a drift in our church today toward severity and away from gentleness. The image that the church, at least the institutional church, so often projects is that of a scolding parent or of the stern, rigid disciplinarian rather than that of the compassionate parent, the caring friend, the sensitive counselor. It is imperative, therefore, that you as catechists serve as an effective antidote to this projection of severity by being people who are approachable, people who assume more a posture of listening than of lecturing, people who are faithful to the teaching and tradition of the church but who are also flexible enough to recognize that this is a living teaching and tradition that must be responsive to the concrete needs and circumstances of each individual to whom you minister.

I would note further that there are three groups within the church that are in particular need of your tenderness and mercy: the poor, women, and fellow ministers. Let me say a word about each.

8. Instruments of Tenderness and Mercy

THAT THE GOOD NEWS is proclaimed to the poor and that the needs of the orphan and widow are met have always been presented in Christian tradition and Christian spirituality as the infallible sign of the presence of God's kingdom among us.

In other words, the way we take into account the poor among us and the way in which they fit into our plan of life tells us a great deal about ourselves and about our own state of spiritual health. Unless we seriously address ourselves to the needs of our suffering brothers and sisters in the world and society around us, we run the risk of losing that which we already have, namely, the right to be sons or daughters of that kingdom founded by our heavenly Father.

If, therefore, we truly believe in God's kingdom and if we are seeking to advance that kingdom in our day, then the poor must rank very high in our values and in our priority system. Otherwise we are deceiving ourselves and it is not God's kingdom that we are advancing but our very own.

That is why our Holy Father Pope John Paul II constantly challenges us to have a preferential option for the poor. We must recognize that a wound in one is a hurt in each, that as long as one child falls asleep hungry at night, my stomach hurts; that as long as an elderly person can't afford heat or fears tomorrow, there is a chill in my bones; or that as long as one person is treated with a lack of dignity, I am ashamed. If one person is treated with a lack of dignity, it is not someone else who is debased or demeaned, but all of us are because this is the nature of the interdependence we have with one another as members of the human family.

It is, in other words, a profound biblical truth that the face of the poor is the face of the Lord. When we cut ourselves off from the poor, we shut ourselves off from the channel of God's grace. On the other hand, when we commit ourselves to serve the poor, suffering, and oppressed, we prepare ourselves for union with our eternal God.

This concern for the poor is particularly critical today, as unfortunately the poor are being made the scapegoats for our socioeconomic woes.

That is why as Christians we must not merely involve ourselves with specific programs that respond to particularized need, but we must also address ourselves to the root causes of social decay.

As Christians, in other words, we must involve ourselves with the messy business of social change. We must be willing to stand with the poor, powerless, and defenseless in their hour of need and not merely be content with applying Band-Aids to deep wounds, or with helping people better adjust to their suffering. We must confront those persons and those institutions that oppress, manipulate, or destroy others, be they the business community, the government, or the church itself. This is precisely what our late Holy Father Pope Paul VI meant when he concluded shortly before his death, "We in the church must shift from a policy which seeks to alleviate the results of oppression to one that seeks to eliminate the causes of oppression."

It is critically important, then, that you as catechists understand this advocacy dimension of the Christian life and communicate it to others. A recent survey indicated that only 38 percent of catechists agree with the statement that Catholic bishops should take a public stance on political issues such as the economy or the arms race, and another survey revealed that only 40 percent of catechists make any effort to get people to think about issues of social justice.

It is vitally important that you catechists be willing to involve yourselves with causes that can benefit the poor: be it opposition to the death penalty, which, where it does exist, is exercised disproportionately among the poor and minority groups; be it health care reform, that seeks to ensure access to comprehensive medical care for all Americans, especially the working and non-working poor; be it challenging zoning ordinances that seek to deny those with AIDS, mental illness, or developmental disabilities or those addicted to alcohol and drugs the right to live in our neighborhoods; or be it familiarizing yourself with the legislative agenda of the National Conference of Bishops or with your state bishops conference that seeks to address the needs of the poor on a wide range of issues such as prenatal care, decent housing, adequate public assistance benefits, or alternatives to incarceration.

As chairperson for the Public Policy Committee of the New York State Catholic Conference, I know full well that when we advocate on behalf of these and other issues with those in state government, they often feel free to ignore our concerns because they believe that we are like generals without armies and thus it won't cost them at the polls. If our Catholic Christian vision and philosophy of life, especially as it pertains to the poor, is to be translated into reality, then it is imperative that catechists like yourselves be aware of the issues confronting our society, be educated on these issues, and be willing through letter or personal contact to let our elected officials know of your support of or opposition to particular public policy concerns.

It should be underscored, however, that your advocacy efforts on behalf of social justice must be rooted in the Gospel of Jesus Christ and the social teachings of the church, which have an originality of their own and must never be confused or identified with any particular political system, economic theory, or philosophical ideology.

I mention this because in advocacy work in behalf of social justice issues, it may come across at times that we in the church are opposed to the government, be it that of our own nation or that of some other nation.

This may be, but if such is the case, the criteria for our opposition as church members must not be based on philosophical or ideological grounds solely, but on the fact that the needs and rights of the poor are not respected and protected.

Furthermore, I think it is evident that advocacy with regard to social justice issues will at times thrust us into the risky area of controversy where we may be challenged, attacked, ridiculed, or ostracized. This is truly the cost of discipleship and of necessity will involve embracing the cross. Failure to place ourselves in this position, however, may well involve complicity with forces and factors that run counter to Gospel values; and this, then, becomes the very essence of social sin.

THE SECOND CATEGORY of persons that should be the beneficiaries of your tenderness and mercy is women. Increasingly, women both lay and religious are finding themselves alienated from the institutional church. More and more women have developed a greater awareness of their unique feminine gifts, talents, insights, and charisms and want to share these more fully with the church. Unfortunately, however, they frequently express a lament that the institutional church is not sensitive to their needs and expectations.

Women have a heightened awareness of being shut out, especially when there is no sensitivity to inclusive language, or when there is no female participation in a liturgy, in roles as lectors or Eucharistic ministers, or when there is no opportunity to serve on important parish or diocesan committees, or when there is no chance for input at staff meetings or on the parish council.

Catechists, then, must be ever conscious of these problems. You must be sensitive to how you might minimize hurts or sleights and be ever willing to affirm the dignity of women and to advocate for opportunities for women to assume positions of leadership and decision-making responsibility within the church — and these opportunities must include programs and funding resources. This was certainly the thrust of the bishops' pastoral statement *Strengthening the Bonds of Peace.*

THE THIRD CATEGORY of persons that should be the beneficiaries of your tenderness and mercy is those with whom you minister in the church, lay, religious, and ordained. For ministry in the church is a shared venture, shared not only in terms of the roles and responsibilities to be exercised but in terms of being affirming of and supportive to one another in our common task of bringing the Good News to God's people.

Yet, unfortunately, too often we who minister in the church are at odds with one another — polarized around labels like ordained and non-ordained, men and women, liberal and conservative — and instead of helping each other, we become pitted against one another. And this antagonism we have for one another in ministry is often the source of great pain and hurt and can be the basis of much deep-rooted hostility, anger, and resentment.

In particular, we in ministry must be attentive to that sin which Monsignor Andrew Cusack calls "lusting of the tongue." By that, he means the terrible violence we do to others by our cruel and cutting remarks.

As ministers in the church we can be hypercritical of one another, especially in talking about one another. I am not referring here to good-natured kidding or poking fun at our human foibles. Indeed, we need to laugh at ourselves and with one another. Perhaps there has been too little of this in our post-conciliar church. What I am talking about is the type of gossip and snide remarks that cut, hurt, alienate, ridicule, and isolate — for example, spreading rumors about another's drinking habits or sexual behavior; impugning motives concerning another's actions or decisions; scapegoating and stereotyping others.

At times such information or such rumors bandied about are blatantly unfounded. Then we are guilty of slander or calumny. At other times the information may be accurate or semi-accurate, but really none of our business or discussed not in a constructive, loving, and caring way but in a way that tears down, that destroys, that debases and demeans someone with whom we share ministry. In any case, such "lusting of the tongue" is not consonant with the example of Jesus who refused to condemn the woman caught in the act of adultery; who refused to label the motives of Zaccheus; who, in his own moment of deep personal agony, refused to ignore the convicted thief who hung beside him on the cross of Calvary.

The old Indian proverb, "You should not judge unless you have walked in another's moccasins," is a piece of advice that needs to be borne in mind. Most times we have no idea of another's pain, of another's struggle, of another's battle with personal demons or human faults and failures.

I have found from both my work on our priests personnel board and now as bishop in a diocese that what frequently appears cut and dried on the surface, in the external forum, may be viewed far differently when people have the opportunity to share candidly from their perspective their quest for wholeness and integrity.

This is certainly not to suggest that we should condone or take lightly behavior that is unbecoming one who ministers in the church, or that we should be unconcerned about another minister who is having a problem. Indeed, we should be concerned, and we have a grave responsibility in this regard. This concern, however, must be constructive rather then destructive. It must involve confronting the person with the apparent problem or confidentially bringing the matter to someone who has the responsibility for addressing such issues. But it should never be handled by rumormongering, witch hunts, or taking glee in another's misfortune.

A few years ago I had a very interesting if somewhat humbling experience that bears out the point I am trying to make. Several of the priests of our diocese attended Father

Charles Gallagher's parish renewal training program. One of the points Father Gallagher makes is that theologically the priest is an extension of the bishop. The bishop, in other words, is the pastor of the diocese and the priest is to be the embodiment of the bishop's presence and ministry in the local parish or institutional situation. Father Gallagher, therefore, maintains that it is imperative that the bishop and his priests be united not only in faith but in love, charity, and understanding as well.

At the conclusion of the parish renewal weekend program, Father Gallagher asks each priest to make an appointment with his bishop. The purpose of the appointment is not only to express loyalty to the bishop and his office but also to ask forgiveness for the unkind things that the priest might have said or even thought about the bishop so that the priest and his bishop might be united fully in mission and ministry. Otherwise, Father Gallagher suggests, the parish renewal itself will be severely impeded.

Needless to say, I had a number of visits. As I mentioned, it was truly a humbling experience to witness the sincerity, the concern, the honesty, and the love of those who came and shared so deeply on a personal level. It was also a very revealing and healing experience. It was revealing because many of the concerns they had about me or my office were things of which I was often unaware — something I might have said or done, something that was said or done in my name, something that hurt them deeply, or something that had put them down and was eating away at them. It was a healing experience because we were able to talk about these hurts, to clarify matters if it was truly a misunderstanding, and to apologize to one another or to ask forgiveness where lack of sensitivity or open communication on either of our parts had inflicted hurt.

It was not always a comfortable or an easy experience to lay these matters on the line. But it was truly a grace-filled moment, a cleansing and renewing opportunity: opportunity to clear the air, to resolve problems, and to re-establish bonds of personal and ministerial support. Where such occurred, I believe, both the priest and I were truly at peace and at one with each other and, consequently, better persons and better ministers because of this reconciling experience.

I strongly encourage you catechists to try to reconcile differences that you may have with other ministers in the church, be these personal differences or differences that may be rooted in varying theological or ecclesiastical viewpoints. If we in ministry are to be reconcilers for God's people, then first and foremost we must make community building, dialogue, and support sharing among ourselves a priority in our ministry. This does not mean that we always have to agree on everything, or that we always have to see things the same way; but it does mean that we must try to understand one another by listening to each other instead of labeling each other and by being sensitive to one another's viewpoints and contributions.

I would suggest that we are all conscious of good intentions as well as of broken promises in this regard. Yet these very past failures and difficulties should impel us to develop the sense of community, the sense of oneness, the sense of mutual support and reassurance that is needed if our ministry is to be the healing, reconciling, and spiritual ministry that God wants it to be and that we ourselves want it to be.

9. Simple Lifestyle

NINTH, CATECHISTS should seek to adopt and maintain a simple lifestyle. In his magnificent encyclical *Centesimus Annus,* commemorating the one hundredth anniversary of Pope Leo XIII's landmark social encyclical *Rerum Novarum,* Pope John Paul II lamented that consumerism that he described as exhausting. He pointed out that we in the West, in particular, are sculpted and shaped from cradle to grave to live and act as consumers. We are bombarded incessantly with high-powered advertising techniques that seek to define and create more and greater need: the superfluous becomes the convenient, the convenient becomes the necessary, and the necessary becomes the indispensable.

Moreover, these high-powered advertising techniques seek not only to create and define more and greater needs, but to shape the attitude and the personality of the consumer as well. The self becomes the center of the universe; other people, things to serve one's needs; the norm, efficiency; the means, whatever works, let the chips fall where they may: unethical business practices, abortion, adultery, euthanasia, or whatever else suits one's convenience.

That is why we need to break away from the lifestyle of high consumption, of wasteful depletion of resources, and of the affluent use of service and leisure that abound within our society, so that we can truly listen to what Gospel values have to say: Gospel values that tell us that we are all God's children and that with respect to the goods of this world we are stewards not masters; Gospel values that say, how blessed are the poor in spirit; Gospel values that remind us that it is easier for a camel to pass through the eye of a needle than for a rich person to enter the kingdom of heaven; Gospel values that tell us that we should be content to be fed and to be clothed.

And while all would readily admit that these are Gospel norms and values, there are far too few people who are willing to take the steps necessary or to make the sacrifices required to translate these evangelical exhortations into lived realities.

For example, the poor person says, "Let the rich begin; I've had enough frugality already." And the rich person says, "Why should I give up what I have legitimately acquired? Besides, if this is going to work, then everyone must be in the same boat. Therefore, let someone else begin and then we'll see." With the net result that no one does anything.

Catechists, therefore, I believe can make a valuable contribution in today's church and society by taking the initiative of offering an irrefutable counterwitness to the consumerism of our day by adopting a lifestyle that enables one to live with what is sufficient; a lifestyle that is less dependent upon status, prestige, influence, and possessions and that is more open and available in service to others; a lifestyle that is characterized by simplicity in clothing, diet, entertainment, and transportation, and by prayers for, advocacy on behalf of, and service to the poor.

And this concern for the poor must extend itself not only to those beset by material need or physical oppression but to those who are spiritually impoverished as well. For the most pitiful form of human poverty is not the deprivation of material goods or possessions but the lack of knowledge of God or the lack of a meaningful relationship with God in one's life. Therefore, you catechists must seek to stir up within yourselves and to communicate to others an awareness of that fundamental human phenomenon that St. Augustine described some sixteen centuries ago and that is equally valid today, "You have made us for yourself, O Lord, and our hearts are restless until they rest in you."

10. A People of Prayer

———— ❧ ————

THIS LEADS to the tenth, final, and most important characteristic that should be the hallmark of the catechist: prayerfulness. As I noted earlier, a major responsibility of the catechist is to be a communicator of God's word: to immerse oneself in the Scriptures, to plunge oneself into the word of God, and to do for teaching what the artist seeks to do for painting and poetry, for sculpture and architecture, for music and dance, for stage and screen, namely, to give God's word meaning and clarity; to tell afresh the story of God's unfathomable love; to bring the mystery of Christ from the Holy Land to our land and to make the Gospel of love real in a setting where you must compete with *Seinfeld, Murphy Brown, ER, Picket Fences,* and *NYPD Blue.*

And you will be able to do this only if you are people of prayer. For teaching is an intolerable burden for the person who is spiritually shallow. Such a person may speak in the name of God while failing to name the experience of God in the life of one's listeners. Such a person may speak of mystery and of all sorts of important things but will not necessarily speak as one personally touched by the mystery of grace or inspired by the soul's thirst for meaning.

It was, I believe, of such a person that Ralph Waldo Emerson wrote over 150 years ago in an address to the graduates of the Harvard Divinity School:

10. A People of Prayer

I once heard a preacher who sorely tempted me to say I would go to church no more. He had no word intimating that he had laughed or wept, was married or in love, had been commended, or cheated, or chagrined. If he had ever lived and acted, we were none the wiser for it. The capital secret of his profession, namely, to convert life into truth, he had not learned. Not one fact in all of his experience had he yet weaved into his doctrine — not a line did he draw out of real history. The true preacher can always be known by this, that he deals out to the people his life — life passed with the fire of thought and prayer.

And what can be said of the preacher can be said of the teacher as well.

Catechists, then, in their lives but especially in their teaching must always come through as people who pray, not a string of

Hail Marys or the recitation of the Divine Office — important as these may be — but as people striving for a ceaseless living in the presence of God.

As catechists, then, you must strive to use the imagination of the novelist and the creativity of the poet to make the word of God relevant to the events of everyday life. But to do this will be possible only if you are steeped in prayer. Indeed to attempt this without being a person of prayer is to bring judgment upon yourself. For as the renowned German theologian Karl Rahner observed, "The word of God in the mouths of teachers empty of faith or love is a terrible judgment. It is already a lie and a judgment upon those who speak what is not within themselves; how much more if they speak of God when they are godless."

Yet despite the obviousness of the fundamental importance of prayer for our life, it seems we can find all kinds of excuses for why we don't have time to pray. Faced with a daily schedule of work and family responsibilities so often we throw up our hands and say, "I just couldn't squeeze prayer in." Or we say, "I pray when I'm driving through town or between appointments or when I'm preparing my lesson." Or there is the famous, "My work is my prayer. At the beginning of the day I offer everything to the Lord and that is how I pray."

While I cannot deny that such can be valid approaches to prayer, I'm afraid that such an attitude or posture may belie the fact that our relationship with the Lord has become lukewarm or that we find time spent with God as fearful or at least uncomfortable. Our situation is not all that unlike a husband and wife who have fallen out of love with one another. So they preoccupy themselves with their hobbies or job responsibilities or the children and grandchildren to overshadow the fact that they have become strangers to one another.

That is why as catechists you must find regular and frequent occasions when you can spend "useless" time with the Lord — time when you can just open yourselves to God in all of your weakness and powerlessness and vulnerability and allow God to be the Lord and to speak to you and to show you in which direction you are to move in your everyday lives.

Finally, for us as Catholic Christians there is one form of prayer that should be preeminent, namely, the Eucharist.

It is at the Eucharist that the church comes together as church. It is at Eucharist that we gain fresh insight about who we are and what we are called to be. It is at Eucharist that we are energized to change our wants, our wills, our loves, and our desires, and if that ongoing conversion that is at the heart of the Christian life does not take place at Eucharist, then it will not take place at all.

Jesuit theologian John Haughey has suggested that there is a phrase we memorialize at Eucharist that can help bring about this conversion: "This is my Body, which is for you." On the night before he was betrayed, Jesus took bread, broke it, gave it to his disciplines and said: "This is my Body, which is for you." "Do this in memory of me." What does this mean? I believe it means that our attitude and our disposition in coming to the eucharistic table must be the same as that of Jesus who said: "I am bread. I am bread broken. I am bread broken for others. Do this..."

A Eucharist then that does not evoke within us a real identification with the other members of Christ's body, others who are in need, others who are suffering, is a Eucharist that is celebrated according to our own mindset and not according to the mind of Jesus. If, therefore, we would celebrate the Eucharist in this radical sense of Eucharist, if at Eucharist we would prepare ourselves to become bread broken for others, then this would substantially alter our understanding of the meaning of ourselves, of our ministry, and of our collaborative relationships with others. It would lead us to change our priorities and to work aggressively to advance God's Kingdom of Peace and Justice in our day.

In his book *A Future to Hope In,* Father Andrew Greeley suggests that we are at the crossroads between pessimism and optimism. On the one hand, given all the advances that have taken place in modern medicine, science, and technology, never before have things looked so good for us. On the other hand, given the moral tone in our world and society, never before have things looked so bleak for us. Greeley states that for the first time in the history of civilization it is truly possible for humankind to recapture paradise — for us to create our own park in which to play or to create hell. The options, he says, are narrowing and by the turn of the century it may well be one or the other: paradise or hell.

What a tremendous challenge and awesome opportunity for you as catechists.

I pray that by rooting your spirituality in the call you have received and the word you are privileged to proclaim and that by seeking to integrate these ten qualities of which I have spoken into your lives, your life and ministry, like the life and ministry of Jesus, may truly give honor and glory to God and living hope to God's people.